Tales of Immigration: Love, Grief, and Resistance in a Foreign Land.

Valery León Quintero

BookLeaf Publishing

India | USA | UK

Presentation by *BookLeaf Publishing*

Web: www.bookleafpub.com

E-mail: info@bookleafpub.com

ISBN: 9789360943950

First edition 2024

*This book is dedicated to my community.
Especially:*

*To Jane Kim for believing and loving me
unconditionally.*

To Tapiwa for his kindness and care.

*To Joë, my person, for being every step in
the past years, from Germany to the United
States.*

*To Wendy for being by my side
unconditionally every day of writing.*

*To Kneeco for listening to my poetry under
the rain and encouraging me to share.*

To Mike Pratt for embracing my creativity.

*To all the loves who broke my heart for
showing me my infinite capacity to love and
care.*

To migrants who deserve a better future.

*To myself and my art, hoping it is the first
and not the last.*

A mi madre, Vero, por su amor.

A mi padre, Hugo, por siempre creer en mis proyectos con amor y en mi primer libro- lo logramos.

A Kyra y a su memoria.

A todes los que nos hemos ido sin irnos.

Most importantly, I dedicate this to love, grief, and resistance of the people.

ACKNOWLEDGEMENT

Tales of Immigration: Love, Grief, and Resistance in a Foreign Land is published during times of collective grief due to multiple genocides actively happening and brutal violence and oppression in my homeland, Venezuela, and the United States. My words honor the grief of those who have been killed and the ones who have survived. My art is nothing if it is not for the people and inspired by them.

PREFACE

When I was 9, my goals in life were big before the crisis. When my life drastically changed when I first moved to Germany, poetry was my only outlet in Spanish while I learned English from scratch. My love and grief were transformed into powerful words that kept me alive. Coming back and leaving for a second time was painful-- I knew it was the last time it would be back in a long time. So, I documented my experiences through poetry, even in the days I thought I would die. Four years later, nearly seven years since I initially left, fluent in English and Spanish, with more than a hundred poems written in my collection, I desperately needed to share it with the world.

Tales of Immigration: Love, Grief, and Resistance in a Foreign Land focuses on my migration process and the different things that have happened nearly seven years since I left my homeland. I centered on grief as the ultimate demonstration of love and a powerful catalyst for resistance. I explore my experiences and how being an immigrant exacerbated elements of heartbreak, grief for lost family members, and falling in love, among others. While I write about my experience, I am inspired by the community of people going through similar situations. Something I learned in the process was that I was not alone. My collection of past and present poems hopes to draw and imagine a future where liberation, justice, and resistance are possible—no human is illegal in a stolen land.

19

It was a dark night
As usual no habia electricidad
It wasn't my first time
And my soul knew it would be my last.
The first time I left
I looked back, knowing they would be there
Then, one by one,
They were taken away.
My friends,
My home,
My safe space.
I left.
Con miedo de volver,
Yo regrese.
But I was not the same person
The 17-year-old who knew well.
I was 19, with shorter hair,
More dreams
And with a little part of me wanting to stay.
Dos meses,
Sixty days
Were enough to realize
I no longer belonged there.
August 19, 2019,
I saw the sunrise,

And my mother's tears hide behind her brown
eyes.
August 19, 2019,
I last hugged my dad for the last time.
19 de agosto,
I left my 19-year-old self,
On the airport line.
I am 24,
And I am 19,
Porque me fui sin irme.

Nowhere

Where do you go
When nowhere is home?
What do you do
When home is just gone?
I am the pain
The one that nothing can alleviate
A miserable fate
Seems to be always there.
Who I become
When I can't be seen
And my light fades away
While I'm alive
Yet feels like death.
You go to nowhere
Everywhere
To the forgotten corners
To the arms of love
You go where you have been
Because pain is something
That gets relieved
Day after day
In violent ways
Yet is better
Than feeling the emptiness
I still wonder

Where do you go
When all you ever loved
Is now gone
Where do you go
When you become a strange
A foreigner in another country
And on your own skin
I say you
Because I can't talk about myself
In a world where I can barely exist.
Where do you go
When the light is off
And not even a miracle
Can save you from the loss
Of your soul
Or your love.
Anyways
Please tell me
Where do you go?

Her

"She is too much," they said
Or she is not as pretty as other girls
They mentioned that "Her life is like a theater
play"
"She has so much drama."
While pretending loving her.

Perhaps her life was a story
or a whole theater play
Deserving of a standing ovation
That had to be shared.

She wakes up
Day after day
With a lot of courage
Trying her best
And making mistakes

She is strong
Fearless
and an incredible girl
When I see her in the mirror
I can't stop thinking
What an honor to be her.

Winter Day

I met him on a winter day
It was one of my good days
I just did not know back then
That the coldest days
Were a couple of months away.
And I got some fresh air
Until the pain drowned me
Deep in the ocean of deaths
Innocent bodies who were not saved
By the negligence of many
And I felt like I was going to lose him
But
How can you lose what you have never had?
And then I moved away
Like I usually do
Because there is nothing more painful than hope.

Time passed by, and one day
He was just in front of me
And I did not know what else to think
Besides, I am so glad you are here.
Since then,
There is no day I have not loved him more.
But hope became more painful than dead
And he will go away

While I pray in silence and wish he is always
okay

I met him on a winter day
And almost a year after
I love him like the coffee in the morning
And taught him the way I break
While running away
Because sometimes the pain
Takes over my chest until I…
I almost lose my breath.
Perhaps is the way I love him
That is inflicting that sense of safety.
I am losing him, and it feels like hell.
I do not want to go back to a winter day.

Dreaming of Returning

A senseless life
Fun, I didn't understand
I was just getting ready
To the day you come back
With all that happiness and love
With all the dreams and songs
With you.
Keeping the same pace to walk
Counting days to hold you in my arms
I kept going and going
Even when my mind was frozen
'Cause you told me that I must never go back
Never go back to the pain
To the cold rain
To tears
I never go back to not being free.
You taught me to hold myself
Strong, close, and tight
So I will keep me safe
I will keep me sound.
Are you going to come back?
Because I can go to you.
Just tell me a day
And I'll come thru.
Wait, but I am here

So are you
'Cause we are the same person
Then we should be the same soul.
I'd never thought to ask myself
When I was coming back
Am I partially dead?
Or am I just taking a trip
With long stops and infinite trains?
So I came back to myself
With a huge smile.
After all, I am missing who I was
All the dreams and all the stars
I'm waiting to come back
And be the same silly
And honest, resilient
The same Valery
That should always come back…

Libertad

Existing
Walking
Inhaling
Exhaling
Oh, my beloved life,
What else can you take apart?

Dreams held at the door,
ready to leave,
are held hostage,
pointed with a gun to their heads.

That is how I get to leave,
with fear of existing,
since the most horrendous crime
is to live
being me.

Thousand of miles away,
I had to learn how to live again,
with an empty suitcase,
and the hope of once coming back
to the home I thought was mine.

I live in "freedom"

daydreaming of coming back,
with the hope that someday,
My Motherland will welcome me back.

Freedom comes and goes as she pleases,
leaving our hearts in pieces,
while we await for her permanent stay,
and the love of her experience.

My life moves
while I am stuck in the past,
thinking of better days,
when I could always come back.

Life is not well lived
until she comes here,
our beloved freedom,
that never dare to exist.

SOY

Soy hija del caos
De placeres y pecados
Con ojos marrones
Ni tan oscuros
Ni muy claros

Mi cabello es un desastre
Pero me encanta despeinado
Y es que así certifico
Que he disfrutado

Viajera permanente
De una maleta color morado
Sueter negro en aeropuertos
Y un pantalón desgastado

De la vida he aprendido
Y sus golpes empeñados
En hacerme crecer rápido
Para no aferrarme al pasado

Tengo una coraza de hierro
Es que soy como un soldado
Pero la hora más oscura
Tengo un corazón desgarrados

Pedacitos de mi vida
En rincones he dejado
Con la esperanza de volver
Y encontrar todo lo olvidado

Me gusta soñar despierta
Y que este todo ordenado
Un cafe negro en la mañana
Con un pan remojao

Creo en la bondad humana
Que no todos somos malos
También creo en los monstruos
Que se esconden en los armarios

No creo en súper héroes
Pero creo que desde el tejado
Puedo ver las estrellas
Y escuchar la risa de un Principito anhelado

Creo en la belleza de la muerte
En el alma de los que amamos
En la necesidad de amar
Y sobre todo, de ser amados

Mis lentes me dan claridad
Para ver todos mis pasos
Aunque siempre titubeo

Nunca echo pa' atrás
Ni me asomo pa' otro lado.

Soy la sonrisa de mi padre
Y la voz de mi madre
Con el aire de un hermano
Y la fuerza de un ángel

Soy tantas cosas
Que desconozco quién soy
Soy un alma sin rumbo
Buscando el camino al sol

Soy el viento que me lleva a dondequiera
Soy la serenidad de la mañana
Y el caos de la tormenta
Soy las estrellas de Sudamérica

Mi voz nunca calla
El sabor de mi tierra no falta
Y lo más importante de todo
Es que soy Venezolana.

Missing Home

Missing home is
Being away for 1668 days
And still feel like it is the first.
Missing home is pretending to be okay
In a place where I am not myself.
Missing home is
Waking up in tears some days
with loneliness pressing your chest
Because you dream of your place
And then you realize you have not been there.
Missing home is traveling places
Figuring out
If you would find yours ever again.
Missing home is
Running away
Because everything has an expiration date.
It is changing every day
Trying to know who you are
Before building who you will be
In a future "so bright"
Yet so empty.
When I miss home,
I travel to my memory box
So I can reconstruct the place
Given that it is not there.

Not anymore.
Missing home is
Talking to my grandma and the stars
And having my brother next to her side
Pretending they are with me
So I do not have another lonely night.
Missing home is
Learning to be apart
Yet, closer than ever,
To a place que ya no está.
Missing home is
Making a home within my skin
So, it does not matter where I am
I am always home,
Even if no one is here.

ORQUÍDEA

*A mi abuela

Flamante amarillo que encabeza tu belleza
y se combina con las alas de cualquier turpial,
pero que solo a ti te lucen
con ese vestido púrpura tan vivaz

Al parecer es una ocasión especial
y mírate deslumbrar,
bailando en el centro de forma angelical
con un ritmo que solo ahora podrás escuchar.

Pequeña flor, no temas en cambiar.
Tus pasos van sin titubear
tan fuertes e incapaz de borrar
y has crecido todo este tiempo para no dejarte
callar,
que nadie arranque tus hojas,
mucho menos dejes que con ellas comiencen a
jugar
Porque tu belleza es flamante
Que solo con ojos de amor hay que mirar.

Pequeña, tu hora está próxima a llegar.
Por eso tan especial te he de mirar

y es que sé que cuando el sol se apague,
ya en otras tierras deberás estar

El sol hoy ha salido
y yo no he dejado de llorar,
Porque el día está más frío
Justo ahora que tú no estás

Por ahí vas
Siguiendo el rumbo de un viento fiestero
Que te mueve al ritmo de un sonero
Ese que tú siempre solías bailar

Espero que sigas volando con tu vestido
Y que tu preciosa magia vaya iluminando cada
lugar
Haciendo dudar al mismísimo sol
Que su belleza es peculiar

Es que te han arrancado mi flor
Para llevarte lejos y esparcir tu olor
Ese que dejaste impregnado con el amor
De una dulce madre que alzó vuelo para ir con
Dios.

(self) love

Forgetting you
A stab in my chest
Pain on my neck
The impossible to say
'Cause I miss you
On every sunset
Or when I drink cafe
While I count stars
Or when I walk in the dark
Thinking of your smile
And your soft hands
Remind me
Of how painful silence was
Is it still?
Quizás sí,
Porque es difícil decidir
Si tu silencio me habla
O si me estás dejando ir
Leaving you is hard
Especially leaving in nowhere
With a few tears left
After I've cried for being with you back them
But wait,
Can you come back once again?
Not to leave stuff unsaid

But to appreciate
The moment I held your soul
And you kept me more alive back then
This is my battle
And I know how sad it became
To fight against me and myself
Once you turned back and left
Pero es una batalla que no quiero
Ni querré
Porque aún en el silencio
Te quiero querer
Pero más que lo que pudo ser
I love myself
I love my fears and tears
I love myself
Pero si tú estás,
Te amo también.

Conocerlo Es Quererlo

Una sonrisa gigante
Que enfrenta a los miedos
Esos que le quitan la vida
Y golpean los sueños

Con pasos tambaleantes
Camina al ritmo del viento
Con un tumbao salsero
Temblando, pero riendo

En el medio de su fuerza
Todos lo ven triunfar
Aunque en las noches
La soledad le ha de golpear

En la esquina de su cama
Sus lágrimas de cristal
Recuerdan que la vida
Se trata de libertad

Amar es libertad
Y la vida es sin sentido si yo no he de amar
A un alma tan noble
Que solo vida puede regalar

Entre tantas piezas
Pronto lograremos (re)ensamblar
Los pedazos de un alma rota
Que solo necesita descansar

Un descanso temporal
Donde nadie pueda atacar
A una simple alma herida
Que está en proceso de sanar

En medio del caos
Llegó a mi vida sin tocar
Una puerta que había cerrado
Cuando pensaba que no se podía más

Bajo la Luna llena
Unidos por el cielo y sus estrellas
Brindamos por la vida plena
Con alegrías y penas

En la distancia celebro
El sentido de libertad
Que me enseñó que para amar
El miedo me he de quitar

Yo amo
Yo amo en libertad
Amo en los atardeceres de verano
Amo a su ser particular

En sus ojos veo
Una vida con miedo
Un futuro con sueños
Un ángel pequeño.

Amar requiere coraje
Y yo lo he de tomar.
Porque incluso sin paracaídas
Del abismo puedo saltar.
Por él
Una y otra vez.
Porque me enseñó que podemos nacer otra vez.

Moon, Sun, and Flowers

She escaped,
had to run away
from the constant death
that was following her
Everywhere.

She moved away
from her known place,
because the worst monsters
are still behind her,
chasing,
running,
not letting her get away.

She is the best
at smiling through the pain
and screaming to the world
with a soft voice
"I am okay."

She is stronger
than anyone else
because no one dares to stop
her extraordinary,
miraculous,

and tremendous grace.

She is an unstoppable flame;
they are so lucky she is contained.
If they saw her in her full self,
they would run away.

She holds the past
of those who never came back
from the trail of death
or the dark path of pain.

She carries love,
patience, and joy,
in every misfortune,
in every heartbreak,
she carries love.

She smiles and the evil,
looking at her,
fades away,
since her existence
is a miracle every day.

She is the reason
I am standing here today.
I always wonder,
how could someone
let her go away,

when she is:
The Sun,
The Moon,
and The Flowers.

Darkest Summer Day

You left us
on a Summer day
the darkest of all of them.
It seemed the world was ending,
since the gray clouds were headed my way.
The rain wasn't coming
because everything seemed okay.
The world wasn't ending,
yet a part of my soul stop moving,
like your little tail.
Everything was so fast,
and I saw my life leaving with you,
and your happy smile,
and the plastic bottles dad made for you,
with the little rocks,
and sticks of wood.
You left with a little bit of us,
and our infinite love.
You left on Summer day,
and months later,
I don't know how to let you go.

Out of everyone,
You were the one
I wanted to come home to.

Out of everyone,
You were the one
Who was happy when I came home.

You are not here,
nor is my home.

Fly high to heaven,
the place where you came from,
You,
Kyra,
My Little,
Sweetest,
and My Kindness Love.

Autumn Day

I woke up today,
I was home again,
looking at the improvised houses on the
mountain,
filled with people like me,
living and surviving
with what they were given.
Mi mami hugged me with a cup of cafecito,
while mi papá was getting dressed,
for the morning walk with Kyra,
my sweet angel,
and return to his juego de ajedrez.

Everything is the same,
it is like I never left,
that little apartment,
where I lost and found myself,
day after day.
Arepas were on el budare,
con huevos en perico en el sartén,
breakfast was almost ready,
and, for once,
we were all there,
together.

From far away,
I could hear the laugh of my muchachito again,
who is taller than me,
but will always be mi bebé.
Happiness filled my heart
until I opened my eyes.

When I opened my eyes,
I was not there,
Home was not an illusion.
I have never been there.
I woke up
on an empty bed,
no coffee was made,
no one was there,
I was alone,
with the grief of the love I left.

I was alone,
on a cold,
silent,
lonely,
autumn day.

Infinite Space

My existence lies between two places
in which none of them I can habit,
and the uncertainty of the future
leaves me floating alone
in a cold, empty,
parallel universe.

My existence became as fragile as the snow,
melting between my fingers,
falling day after day,
without an specific arrival place.

Sometimes darkness makes its way back
to get me where I was before,
and even when I try to stick around
for something I have lived for,
nothing is like it seems.

I dream of the places
where I was happy one day.
The land is my Mother,
and criminals kicked me away.
I moved to another stolen land,
where people like me,
have to fight a chance to exist,

to resist.
A stolen land,
where genocide is televised,
while any resistance,
is criminalized.

Then, in the parallelism of universes,
I dream of places
where I thought I was fully myself,
and in this lonely world,
love creates the illusion,
that I am never alone,
so I do not have to run away.

My existence is everywhere and nowhere,
in the infinite space of love,
resistance,
and liberation,
in the ephemeral moment of happiness
my mind creates
hoping that one day,
I find the person I am,
within others,
in this infinite space.

Until the Next Day

There is something special
in the sense of pain;
it distorts the way we see,
because what it is,
it is not what it feels.

Pain is like running barefoot,
on December 23rd,
because it is -1°,
but it feels like -20°.

Everything is normal,
and I still wonder
what is everything?
If the world is falling apart,
so many have died,
and so many left to die,
how can we just all be here?

The miracle of pain
grows in such a way
in which you are forced to create,
to live,
to breathe,
even when everything is going away,

and blood is everywhere.

It is that type of pain
that teaches you
on a cold winter day
you can still run
and enjoy the fresh air,
and the reflection of the Sun,
because, soon,
it will go away,
like everything and
everyone else.

When everything falls apart,
we can build it again,
in a different way,
so we transform the pain in love,
resistance and care.
We let it go away,
until the next day.

Mi Alegría

35

Tus ojos,
tu sonrisa en sincronía,
con el ritmo de la música,
y todo parece poesía.
Mi vida,
esa que dejó de ser mía
el día en que decidiste
ser mi eterna compañia,
en las noches más vacías,
en los días soleados,
y en las tardes frías.

Tus ojos
y tu sonrisa:
fuentes naturales de vida.
Oh, vida mía,
eres tú,
solo tú,
eres mi alegría.

The Moon (She/Her) on a Summer Day

The sunset was leaving
as cars passed by
and the Moon kept me company
until the moment She went away
the same way they did,
the same way I do,
in silence,
accustomed to the pain.

Even the Moon goes away.

When it is time for Her to be there,
I know she is there,
just looking at someone else.
I am left to pray
that She comes back,
again,
later today,
to tell me stories,
or the next day.

When only a few hours of the night are left,
I tell the stars,
that I will always be looking after Her.

I have told the starts
I will always
In every day
will be looking for Her.

Saudade

El alma está vacía
y hoy es de esos días donde suelo dudar
si ha habido algún habitante
y en donde ha podido estar.

Estoy cansada de buscarlos,
de solo soledades encontrar
en un espacio vacío
y con una tristeza tocando a la puerta para entrar.

Mi memoria comienza a trabajar,
ojos marrones que comienzan a destellar,
otros azules que quieren opacar
y unos verdes que mueren otra vez por estar.

El alma está vacía,
ninguno de ellos está.
Trato de amarrarlos,
mi cuerda se desato y ellos ya no están.

Sus ojos azules
simbolizan el agua del mar,
esa tan cristalina
que su pureza puedes respirar.

Me he quedado sin mar y sin cielo,
sin un pedazo de hogar
siendo eso lo que más le duele
a una persona que ya no puede llorar.

Su mirada café me despertaba
 y justo ahora que no está
mi cama no he vuelto a tocar
y si lo hago será para jamás despertar.

Deseo despertar en la selva
verde como su mirar
para recordar cuanto le amaba
a ver si algo de ella vuelve a llegar.

Sigo sentada
esperando y con un fuerte palpitar
de que jamás regresarán
Y que jamás ese amor volverá.

Me he secado de llorar
y es que también me he cansado de vomitar
ese remolino de emociones
que todavía no deja de estar.

Estoy liviana porque llevaron todo de mí,
arrancaron todo mi sentir
Me dejaron apenas vivir
sin saber cuán doloroso sería por ellos sufrir.

No volverán jamás
y no tuvieron la decencia de limpiar
los recuerdos más clavados
en una pared que ahora me toca reparar.

Han dejado mi hogar
y eso que yo nunca les di permiso de entrar,
se han ido para no regresar
y es algo que no puedo cambiar.

se fueron de puntitas,
sin zapatos y con un sigiloso respirar,
para hacer el menor ruido
y así dejarme sin despertar.

Ellos despertaron el infierno,
el desgarro de saber que jamás van a regresar,
ese al que hoy me enfrento,
ese que se ha querido quedar acá

Le doy la bienvenida,
él solo me ha de mirar,
sintiendo gran lastima
incluso cuando todo el caos era de esperar.

Él me ha dicho que me han dejado
y yo al recuerdo no me puedo aferrar
es que mis fuerzas las he dejado

en las maletas de los demás.

Llego el momento de ver las estrellas,
de entender que sola voy a estar
porque se han llevado la vida
y risas para acompañar su caminar.

Se han llevado tanto de mi
para no quedarse solos,
sin saber que sigo aquí
y que no cambiará de ningún modo.
Vaya que tristeza inunda mi alma,
vaya que añoranza suele arribar
a un pobre corazón
que ha aprendido a esperar.

Me quedo con el respirar de su cuello,
con el café mañanero a medio terminar,
con memorias efímeras
que espero sean largas e imposibles de olvidar

Y si yo llegase a olvidar quienes me han dejado,
ellos habrán de regresar
para enseñarme que lo mejor de la vida es amar
y recordar,
que añorar duele,
pero es mucho mejor que no tener a quien
extrañar
y que el amor todas las fronteras suele quebrar.

Blooming Spring

Every day a battle takes place
to transform the pain
into the red roses
I always wanted,
because time slips through the hands
of the one who never gives up
and maintain the hope
so life can move on.

Roses are blossoming every day
for the broken hearts
of those who loved unconditionally
and life failed them.

Sometimes, one needs to fall apart
to heal a broken heart
and pretend it is okay.
Hopefully one day
a garden full of roses,
blooming on a warm Spring,
will be a reminder that
eventually
it will be okay.

Gracefully Existing

Our bodies became an extension
of a revolutionary way of existing,
because we resist the oppression
while we fight the system
that keeps telling us
To go home because we do not belong.
And we struggle to say
the jungle was safer than the home we had
known for so long.

When our mere existence
bothers the system
of oppression and exploitation,
when our bodies
become another point of data
we know that it does not matter.
Neither in our homes
or the 'Land of the Free'
We cannot peacefully exist.

While they ask us
to go back,
because 'we steal'
and 'we do not belong here'
We remember that,
on behalf of 'freedom',

and to protect capitalism,
Genocides on this land,
and beyond,
have been committed.

We are not only refugees;
Asylum seekers;
'Aliens.'
We are People.
We are Communities.
We are the Sea that held our bodies;
The Jungle that brought us alive.
We are the pain of those who tried to make it
but couldn't survive.
Because home is a city on fire
It is the chaos itself.
It is the land that saw us come to the world,
then forced us to leave,
and told us never to look back again.

Our bodies are extensions of love,
extensions of the days
that seemed so normal;
yet, they were never the same.
Because when our homes were invaded,
destroyed and thrown away.
No one stood up for us

and we had to escape.

When we are targeted
labeled as the 'aliens' of this land,
We chose to continue existing
and giving back
to Communities that need us.
We chose to be lights
in the face of darkness,
because we know that home
one day
could go away.

No one leaves home
to navigate an uncertain sea.
No one leaves home
to run through the jungle and face the beast.
No one leaves home
unless there is nothing else to lose.
No one leaves home
unless home has left them alone.

Our bodies became an extension
of a revolutionary way of existing.
We resist the oppression
Our bodies became an extension
of the love that we have been missing,
because there is nothing that bothers them more
than us, gracefully existing.